THE THIN LIGHT OF WINTER
New and Selected Poems

Jonas Zdanys

The Thin Light of Winter was published in Chicago
on December 21, 2009, the Winter Solstice, by
VIRTUAL ARTISTS COLLECTIVE
http://vacpoetry.org

ISBN 978-0-9819898-1-5

Poems in this selection have appeared in the following books, anthologies and journals, some of them in somewhat different versions: "The Woman on the Bridge" appeared as a limited edition chapbook published by Virtual Artists Collective. "Two Seasons in the Orchard" appeared in *Freshwater*. "This Morning," under a different title, was published as a memorial broadside for the fortieth reunion of the New Britain High School Class of 1968. "The Dry Season" appeared as a pamphlet published by Red Pagoda Press and in *White*, published by The White Birch Press. The sections of "Bones" included here first appeared as part of a sequence of the same name in *White*, together with "Spring Perspective," "Light," "A Poem in Honor of Li Po," "The Door," "Immortality," The Solstice, Early Morning at the Window," The Last White Blinding Radiance," "Excerpts from the Autobiography of a Man Who Casts No Shadow," "Inscriptions in the Margins...," and "Confession." "November Song" originally appeared in Lithuanian and in a somewhat different version in *Dūmų stulpai* published in Vilnius by the Lithuanian Writers Union Publishing House. "The Angels of Wine" appeared in *The Poetry of Men's Lives: An International Anthology* published by the University of Georgia Press. It, together with "Lithuanian Crossing," "His Father's Son," "Rhapsody," "A Physical Phenomenon," "The River," "Entering the Tiny Kingdom," "The Word," "Undeveloped Photographs," "Epiphany," "West of San Juan," "Interior with Faded Colors," "First Light," "The Sound," "The Lace Maker," "October Garden," "Vermont Morning," "The Things of the Eye," "The End of Mythology," and "The Ghost in the Kitchen" appeared in *Lithuanian Crossing* published by The White Birch Press. "Priam's Daughter" first appeared as an illustrated broadside published by The Blue Newt Press and was staged as a dramatic choral reading at the Beinecke Rare Book and Manuscript Library of Yale University. "The Metaphysics of Wolves" was published as a hand-made letterpress edition by The White Birch Press. "St. Francis at Alverna," "Seeing Wyeth's *McVey's Barn* Seventeen Years Later," "Inheritance," "Freight Trains," "My Father's Wine," "February Snow," "Raking," "Christopher's Dream," "The Shadow of Death on the Open Water," "Easter Morning," "Chiaroscuro," "Simple Gestures," "A Point of Departure," and "Winter Geese" appeared in *Water Light* published in Vilnius by Vaga Publishers, Ltd. "Maine Aubade" was published as a chapbook by Appletree Books. "Love," "North Light," "10th Avenue," and "Block Island Blues" appeared in *Voice on an Anthill* published by Manyland Books. "The White Bend of the River" was published as a hand-made letterpress illustrated and numbered edition at the Carl Purington Rollins Press at the Yale School of Art.

The cover is a photograph by the Dutch artist Ineke Kamps titled "Speckles of Dust." It is used with the kind permission of Ineke Kamps, whose work may also be found at: http://www.inekekamps.nl The cover design is by Algis J. Kalvaitis. The two section illustrations are by the Lithuanian artist Romas Orantas and originally appeared in a volume of my poems in Lithuanian titled *Aušros daina* published in Kaunas by Santara/Spindulys. They are used with his kind permission.

for my daughters

Contents

New Poems

IN THE LAND OF BLUE SNOW

1.

after Henrikas Nagys

We trace the child's face in the first snow.
My sister sleeps under wild raspberry branches.
Last night someone spread light snow
on frozen ground white as my mother's hair.

We trace my brother's face in the first snow.
The guard's epileptic daughter crumbles
dry bread on the echoing ground.
We hear it fall as the wild clouds bleed.

Birds carry moonlight on their frozen backs.
Beneath the ice rivers flow slowly to the sea.
My sister's doll sleeps under wild raspberry branches.
We trace my brother's cold face in the blue snow.

2.

There are no trees in the land of blue snow:
only the shadows of trees, the forgotten names of trees.

In the hall of cold mirrors dead fingers trace
the breath of silhouettes on dusty glass.

In the land of blue snow only words remain,
lines and letters drawn in cool ash and sand.

Look: above my face old snow is falling:
the sky so white, and the voices of black birds.

———

3.

A dog was barking outside
and the streets filled
with the slow orphans of wind.

Clouds swallowed the ghost light
of the sky, crumbling to coils
sharp as needles of ice.

The ransomed shadows of evening
framed her face, a black snag
of lightning on the horizon.

We hold our tongues, the earth's
white scar, and the cold breath
of snow recongregates all morning.

4.

We dig roots out from under half-buried rocks,
pull thorns from sorrowful water.

The sky is transformed to porcelain and black crystal,
unfaithful at last.

Weightless air splashed on blue snow, the insignificance
of night and the flash of late stars.

Solitude easy as the red moon outside the window, the promise
of clouds and a light wind from nowhere.

And I shake loose at the margins, unencumbered and free:
a whisper, a flicker, a spark.

———

5.

This is not a trick of light but the cross of wild rails,
ice that sculls the hills in a gaze of slow air.

A membrane of many angles undeveloped
by feeling or time, the sky a dry wound,

the silence before this longing, this terrible sadness,
this slow unlocking of the cadenced night began

in the unanswered clarity of brilliant forms,
in the deepest blue of the coldest snow.

6.

When the time comes they'll bring you to a place like this,
to sleep as you have always slept, invisible and still,
after the long years have split the great meadow
and the city's streets have run away in all directions
and the space in which you wanted to live is filled.

The satisfactions of another year, dust on the sill,
the night like water and the enfolding light.
You have arrived at last and the blue snow scatters.
Tomorrow you will be different again. Try to remember
your name, take your turn at the window.

7.

The month gone, those sad marks,
the clarity of north wind
blue as the snow that rises to meet it —
and the fire dances
between darkness and light,
makes a sound so thin
I kneel to find it.

8.

By midnight dreaming of trees and last year's apples flaked with snow.
The stillness in the gathered dark, healed wounds and imperfections,
feeling your absence with my own hands, the emptiness
that hangs like the cold ache of an old thread in the night wind.

The earth here follows you, unties the sorrows of your heart.
Turn your back, fly straight into the sun.
Don't be afraid of the last sounds, your face, small and low,
infinity tapping like blue snow on your closed eyes.

9.

I have considered such things often
in my oldest nights, the full moon shining —
how we stood at the window
looking out at the snow,
how her fingers touched my hair.

It had more to do with snow than love,
the thread of something important,
the noises in the street, and if we spoke
it was in whispers, and the room
subsided, and she sank in a long sigh.

It was a simple thing. And when she left
I was caught between the earth and air.
I was both halves of myself: part water,
part glass: the thin light of winter,
the fine dust of the year's last song.

10.

The place is forgotten now. While the snow fell,
slow and immeasurable, the moon mirrored
in the ice and the house so quiet as she slept,
the light and shade where other lovers played.

Taste the unhurried snow. Stop as the pale wind stirs.
The whole world will happen again, rising
out of itself for the last time as memories
and mute desires swing dark and away.

Forget these words, calm your fears, breathe deeply.
Hold the moment that opens before us:
in the weight of things, in the faint blue light
of the dream's last hour, life sings itself out to the end.

———

THE WOMAN ON THE BRIDGE

1.

It is a long path of laid cinders and stones
curving past the small spaces between white trees.

Up ahead are the ripples and curls of a river
below a dark stone bridge.

Flurries of dust and loose dirt sift
in patterns on the stones of the road.

The horizon hangs low above the bridge
and its brown wooden railings and posts.

I see her from a distance, dressed in a short coat
and skirt the same color as the bridge.

She stands at the near end as I approach,
presses her face close, calls me by another name.

Something falls from the sky.
Time breaks.

The black flowers at the bottom
of the bridge suddenly blossom.

2.

Night has already fallen.
I light a lamp for her in the dark room
but she pushes me away.

I adapt without complaint to this new pattern.
I sleep fitfully
and when I wake my hands are cold.

Morning comes tapping at the window,
moves erratically from point to point
in the empty room.

———————

3.

There seems to be time for all things,
time enough for everything,
even for the silence between us.

I rise and follow her across the yard
to the cinder and stone path that leads to the bridge.

I am aware of the vastness of the sky above me.

She holds out her hand to me
offering something,
all feathers and bone,
a soul stirring its wings.

On the bridge I have no fear now.

If I fall into the air I know I will float away,
receding, separated, drifting.

4.

The hours pass in a flat hard place
without shadow or depth
and time is dry as paper.

This morning I do not know
if it began or did not begin
or the possibilities of abstraction.

The body grows silent
among the changing echoes
of what was.

The shifting light
of all that has disappeared
beyond the hope of what will come.

Perhaps in time
I will learn
to howl at the moon

watch birds
settle to roost
as light thickens on the bridge

skip over
entire days and nights
as if they never happened.

Space decomposes and recomposes itself
before my eyes
as I move down the slope to the river.

5.

It was how the story ended:
sand already in the boy's mouth
settling in, claiming him

carrying him
through the shallows
into the darker depths,

part of his essence
not here but in the future
like a shadow cast before him,

the dark haze of hope
he can never catch
as his trembling at last subsides.

A fly settles on his cheek,
cleans itself,
circles and settles again.

6.

She asks me
why I live
in the green hills

I smile
I do not
answer

I am completely at peace

a blossom
floats past
on the current below

I tell her
there are worlds beyond this one
among the white stars

7.

A day must have passed,
must have intervened here,
something must have changed,

but I don't trust
such suppositions,
am impatient with the flow of time.

Sunlight pours through the window
onto an empty bed.
The door is locked.

I help her undress
in the airless silence
of this place, my heart quickens

as her brown skirt falls to the floor,
a suspension, a moment
before the return of time.

Her body is mapped with the signs
that she is beyond her term,
eternal, thrashing about, transparent

struggling for air
in the faint turbulence
of the time that passes.

———————

8.

It is time for what comes
out of the ashes to come.

Time for that which shows
through the flesh.

This is how the trap is laid,
how they are caught.

The dry earth soaks up
the blood of its creatures, never sated.

If this is my fate I'd rather be
a stick in an empty field.

On the far side of the bridge
something pale stands out against the sky.

It will be a difficult day,
a day for waiting.

9.

They have made a room without a window.
I cannot see but I remember how

morning after morning the day passes,
dusk falls, and then darkness comes.

Here, someone switches on the lights
and there are dissatisfied murmurs all around,

discontent at the dissolution of the membrane
between the world and the self inside.

I must have slept. When I opened my eyes
she was kneeling beside me, feeling under the quilt.

For a while I was nowhere, shook my head,
this is my hand, I say, this is the bed, this the floor,

my soul alert, darting, and in the morning
when she reemerged at the edge of my oblivion

swirls of mist floated past her, a dark speck
moving against the stillness of other dark specks,

embraced the bridge and floated away
with the spirits and wraiths,

---

the great beam of my vision illuminating
the helpless complicity of all who watched,

all they said to one another in this windowless room
in the closest dead of night.

Days and nights wheel past as the lights in the room
brighten to gray-green and then darken to black.

In a week or a month I will
have forgotten everything,

will look around intently and no longer know
who waits for me to step into the shadow.

10.

Heavy rain sheets over the edges
of the roof, swirls of water on the grass
and trees just visible through the window.

The earth returns into itself
and the leaves fall and the stars dip
low in the clouds on the horizon.

I think of you on the bridge, wound together
a thousand times, and feel the stirring
of the air as I call to you in the dark.

This is the grace of things to come,
the one sorrow I walk through in my sleep,
the shine I move toward as the wind shifts.

The rain is the only line drawn between us tonight.
The veil of grayness outside the window grows lighter.
Out ahead, the pale blue of farther skies.

11.

When time drifts like a heavy truth
across the bridge
and the sky comes down
and covers me completely

I am held by nothing and hold on
to nothing, see nothing inside of nothing,
sit bewildered like the man who wondered
all his life and discovered and then forgot

the hidden meaning of things
set loose in the landscapes of sheer earth
in moments of no importance
that spill themselves like dry leaves

and move from one stillness to another,
to the indecipherable taste
and bitter dust
of dry seasons kept from decay.

Revelation, intuition, inspiration:
it would be better to be an empty mind,
the dull and dimly lit, than to live
with the weariness of this uncertainty,

---

to be neither still nor in motion,
neither force nor will, not dream or guess,
but everything at once, the eternal now,
where nothing returns and nothing repeats,

searching for the metaphysics of the spirit
not the small realities of the body,
the swift-colored thing that passes
in canceled desires and the rising of the dead,

not knowing and not keeping,
dissolved to a drift of smoke
as the moon swings dark and away
and the sky withers and the ash falls.

I have considered such things often,
have fallen with the weight of things
everywhere and unobserved,
have understood how it all begins:

at night when the lights come on
and life changes its face
in every crevice and corner,
I see her in the distance on the bridge

breathing the last breath of dusk,
pointing with unmistakable clarity
to what we had come for as the wind shifts
and darkness invades the day.

12.

There is magic in this world I'll stand where
I'm standing now here on the dark porch

The spirit moves forward and the self persists
where the winds and waters meet

I stand outside myself the finite in the infinite
under the rock at the white shore

I have seen what I have seen the mind in the air
the swift tide of longing the clean tear

The joy of being the sigh of the soul pale body
and the naked ease of myself

The word made word and flesh thick waters dropped seed
the blue expression the whole of light

Where the river lies still clear night telling who comes and goes
the breath's moment that moved on

Time folds and the sounds I hear in this vulnerable place
tell of dust leaves ash idea revelation

———

13.

We let the day take us where it wants
like a slow shifting of the bridge.

Just beyond the gate
everything stays as it is.

The straight trees the curved sky
the slow falling rain.

Day after day
nothing repeats itself.

The window reflects a chair a lamp
a changing moon.

The end of it all weightless the sky the eye sees
the landscapes of the past it cannot find.

The light begins to thin the light we move toward
all dust and colorless moan.

We are the last to leave
after all the others have left.

We stand on the other side
whispering something.

14.

I dreamed of being lost and covered with leaves.

I woke up shouting, my throat full.
It was night again and I licked the mirror
into which I was staring clean.
White light reflected in shards of glass
on all sides and in a minute all was done.

I have gone over that moment a thousand times
in my mind, have thought about it for a thousand moments:
it was a sadness, a pillar of smoke dry as the world
around my neck, a disturbance of the soul,
all lightness gone, the desperate silence of a deserted house,
and I understood that I am the last of my kind,
living in the old way, drifting through time:
even if I lay low and breathe quietly
they'll hear my heart beating, clenching
and unclenching like a stranger's fist in my chest.

I no longer know what to do with my face.
The sun had set, the wind began to bite,
a half moon was coming through the clouds.
I took the old road, waving my arms,
and inside my head I heard the green music.

No one is forgotten.
In a moment of astonishment
I tumbled into the cauldron of history

———

and saw the burned posts of the bridge,
the vast airiness of space between heaven
and the green lines of the river,
the outlines of the words of love
she mouthed to me soundlessly there.
I felt the shame of private knowledge,
the moral dimension of my plight.

I am drowning,
arguing with cold clarity
for all that is unheard,
gripping the bars of the gate.

I listened
and nodded
and dreamed,
shivering with cold,
and my fingers
would not
straighten.

Something has fallen on me.
I crept away, touching the silence
of airless places, was pulled this way
and that by the shrunken tug of the moon,
leaped and groaned at the far edges
of the sky, watched patterns
of chaos manifest themselves
as moments of transfiguration.

I welcomed that dissolution,
pondered its sounds.

_____

Night pushed a stick into my mouth,
left its thin black mark on everything.

Tomorrow will be a new day.
Tomorrow will not be today.
Today I am so tired that I reel on my feet,
wriggle and sob like a frightened child.

I am hollow:
unthinking, inarticulate, without imagination:
I come to speak but have nothing to say:
today is the day but today has passed:
how will I know how I lived in this place, in this time:
swept over the brink, a cold wind blowing,
rain falling on barren soil.

An hour must have passed
or the blink of an eye:
events overtook me:
the spark flickered and lost itself at once.
I followed the reflected light,
crystalline and bloodless,
and gripped the earth to steady myself.

The thought began to float away but I clung to it:
there will be another time, and if not, then I don't mind:
I am a blind man dancing, as if in another country,
struggling for a foothold in unfamiliar sand.

All my life I waited for someone to call to in the dark.
I see them I call out *here here I am here*.
They skulk in the open, stand in a circle around me,
don't know what to say or do.

I am, to some or to many, the beast
that stares out from behind the gate
or from across the bridge,
an unborn laboring creature,
the obscurest of the obscure.
I whisper and tumble free as the odor of smoke.
I stumble and fall, reach out a slow hand,
wince at the sharpness of the light.

The fear of the past day has lost its tense.
I will defend the cause of justice,
the precious safety of the fragile and the liquid-eyed,
will forever shake off the weight
of the resentful gazes that rest on me,
will say my part, will understand how to speak of this.

God's time is not our time.
I dream but I don't think
I dream of God
or that God dreams of me.
I dream that there is water everywhere,
paths that lead nowhere:
holy ground:
resurrection from the earth:
the soul emerging, a creature of air:

———

truth frozen in its tracks,
the future disguised
in the name of some present abstraction.

The wind dropped, the air was clear.
The silence was so dense, there was nowhere to hide,
and the ground sighed as my body returned
not to the great cycle but to the jagged time
of rise and fall, of start and finish, of beginning and end.

Time stopped and then started again.
I did not want to be drawn away,
struggling and lost, gesturing from horizon to horizon
in joy or lamentation, living between reason and truth
in a secret life I do not see or understand,
a spirit invisible, but the vision faded
and the dust came and the leaves.

15.

Tomorrow
when the war ends
when the moon seeps like dust
through the crack in the door
and draws the fictions of our souls

Tomorrow
when we hang our lives
in the attics of old houses
and fragments of time
are like a knocking on the wall

Tomorrow
when we see dead faces
in the mirror on the pillow
and feel the brevity of our days
in the window and water below

Tomorrow
when we repeat the sounds
of the letters of our names
and touch the thinnest edge
of the voice of God

Tomorrow
when the haze in me lifts
when every hour is mine

and the song of the infinite
is like a silence of the heart

I will empty the drawers
undress bathe breathe go out
sketch the anguish of regret
redeem myself feel the pain of separation
complain softly rise up float across the skin of the earth
feel the scales thicken fan my wings
pause stare out into the distance
render myself into words
let go of myself let go of you
be stunned astounded free of feeling
be turned to stone see the long night ahead
sleep dream wake wait until tomorrow

16.

That year there was no spring.
After winter came winter.

The air grows dry and light
by late December as the heaviness of fall
slips away into the folding corners of the sky.

The day passes uneasily, the simplicity
of the moment passes, and time flows
like a snapped twig on the current under the bridge.

I am whole inside. I speak a language
of distance and perspective, though I have
no words to explain why my bones grow cold.

I can run away, emptied of secrets, utter
my life in words no one else understands,
or sit in the corner with my mouth shut.

I am beyond name and form,
stillness and movement together,
and when I see God I will be very small.

It is a confession I am making here:
I am asleep with no sense of time
and dream that the moment of waking is at hand.

———

The flow has ceased. Winter is coming again.
A cold wind whistles across the bridge.
A thin sheet of ice covers my face.

17.

The yard filled with smoke and then
the rooms of her house. I go outside.
Time slows, the horizon lifts.
The trees are indistinct black smudges
against the enveloping gray.

I close my eyes, feel my way inside
with the fingers of my hand. Life is
ordinary again. She sits in the corner
working but does not see me,
pale as old bones in dry light.

I lay my head on my arms. Night filters
through the window: embers of trees and
burned grass without substance or form.
The future invades my mouth, quivers
like the empty smell of smoke in the room.

There was a long silence. She says she is
a drop of water, a colorless bird, a piece of glass,
a cry in the dark, flesh of my own flesh,
and asks me to give her my fingers, one each day,
and let her stretch her life across to the far shore.

I will never be warm, I think, *I will never be warm*,
the thought coming and going like a wild piercing
of the smoke, blood and earth, a sudden stirring
of life in the womb. In an instant I am gone
and in another I am back again, facing the wall.

18.

There was a smell of wet ashes in the air.
I cross to the window. It was nearly dark.

The world outside was blackened with burning,
moonlight and briny ice. Today is the day.

I am standing by the river, waiting for someone
to show me the way across. Truth without flesh.

The month is gone and the day. A woman's cycle.
I am standing by the window. It is nearly dark.

There is no one here. I am already across the water and home.
I was bowed under the weight of the day. I am lost.

I kept my vigil for a day and night. It was nearly dark.
I returned to the riverbed. The flames flow from me.

They burned the thought of something of water that stands and runs.
Before this longing the flames in one small fire, the eyes vague.

Light paints the walls black as old splinters. It is nearly dark.
Wind cuts the yellowness of my solitude on the gray road home.

I have fallen and she catches me. Tense, resistant, hard.
Now there is nothing to hold her. After a while I was still.

The smoke dissolved and the heavens opened and the light
burns down penetrating and sharp. My voice tastes like wet ashes.

I yield to this contagion. The ghosts are gone. It was nearly dark.
They fall and are washed away before they cross. I howled at the moon.

19.

All things are possible at the same time
everything from all sides
and nothing needs to be done.
I have seen all things.
I have witnessed nothing.
I have been around every corner.
I have been inside every wall.
I have failed in everything, in nothing.
I have returned from everywhere.
I have loved everyone, and hated.
I have seen my face in all faces.
I look at life passing by.
I am blind and deaf.
I see and hear everything.
I wait for what I do not know.
I am beginning to know myself.
I divide what I know, everything that exists, exists.
I am now and everything I never will be.
I am living right now.
I walk by, everything's hidden in the night that remains.
I lie down in the grass.
I am the landscape, the sky and air.
I think about nothing.
I speak I stop seeing her I write I forget myself.
I am the bridge, I am the sky, the first and final star.
I pick the black blossoms stirring my wings.
I am naked and plunge into the water.
I feel the edges of the world.

———

20.

Below the root the water knows my name

its delicate hesitations
drained dry as seasons drift and go

cold winter
salt and flesh and the river falls
running down and standing still
against the panes of the wind

invisible at night
splashing the lunar sky
its glide breaking the erratic ice

between the surface and the slate-colored bottom
the shapes that cannot be seen

fresh weavings
of earth and air
over the snow at night
and the ghosts of the heart
in the ripening light

———

NOCTURNE

1.

after Nijolé Miliauskaité

I know a place where when you
brush your foot across the sand
the sand moans sadly
as if weeping

sometimes
a woman appears there, dressed in black
with eyes emptied of tears

wind carries her across the sand
like the shadow of a cloud

blows through her hair forever

2.

Night and a weightless moon
washed cold and white as a dying star –
to lie naked in the sand,
hear the silence above the sunken tree,
rise and fall in the long moment,
slip through the slide and ache
of your heart and feel the slow pulse
in the hand of God as it touches
your face in the lingering hour.

3.

It was the only way it could be known —
the secret when the world began,
the centuries of dust, small things
sleeping forever in the earth,
the dry road, the shattered glass,
the withered white of a single day.

And everything then seemed a single day —
the pain she felt, life on all fours,
a wrinkle in the sand, as the old men say,
collisions in the clouds, the dark stones
underground coming up and out
the way her soul might rise.

4.

Silence on your eyelids, clouds on the fragile face of the day.
Old roses in late September, petals falling and falling.
The night's slow song, the moon spread across the cold of morning.
The moment of turning, become another thing, as the ground clears
and the roots climb. Your grief that day was something like this,
your prayer rising to heaven, sand the color of nothing
sifting through your hand as it clenches and unfolds.

———

5.

Up ahead, a few more hours along the empty road.
The night sky blind as heated metal.
A flock of black birds in the distance waking the landscape.
An unfamiliar hand brushes across your back
under a white half moon hanging in the dark clouds:
a girl in a white dress, the shake of her voice
as she offers water to the dying, to you, the dry grass
rustling as she passes, the smell of cold air
on the line of horizon calling her home.
You sit on the road, resting, waiting.

6.

I stand by a low wall
indifferent to the stars
and watch all night.

She passes by like a thing
thrown into the air,
a little square
of fading black cloth.

In another world then
as now, the lapse of time
as I look toward morning
and see salvation.

Overhead,
the light of oncoming rain,
the sky fragrant and close.

Two Seasons in the Orchard

1.

So little remains at the center of things as day settles
into a corner of the sky letting go of its colors:
a small enclosing darkness filled with uncertain shapes,
a pale light that unexpectedly brushes the water,
a sudden memory of thin clouds scudding east
in the late summer night and the look
in your eyes when a vein of blue skimmed the pond
and I touched you for the first time, damp
with the cool smells of apples in this sweet orchard grass.
That memory comes and goes with a slant of light
the color of dry leaves that holds the afternoon like
a meditative hand before sheeting to dusk. Its shadows
simmer soft as the grayness that clings to the edges of water.
This night, low clouds pass across the pond
with the nesting birds, weaving their grizzled hues
along the horizon, and the cadence of the season
floats blank and troubled on a rising wind.

2.

Time drifts like water on drying glass and leaf
by leaf the trees chip themselves to winter.
Light falls to carved shadows delicate as the air
before sunset, fixing to perfect lines on the water.
Night comes in clouds tangled as soft roots
that loosen above apple trees rubbed to autumn
and late flowers hiss and bloom unexpectedly in the dark.
These are the risks we are born into,
possibilities that flutter to uncertainty in the night air
like birds lifting from the weeds in sudden flight
and spilling to broken circles across the dimming sky.
The moon rises sheer and gray as a shiver
of recognition and the image of your face pressed
in the grass beneath these trees washes through
the brown weeds around me with the sound of wings,
scattering into the distance like brittle leaves
or dust caught in a chill confusion of wind.

THIS MORNING

This morning, the house rests in the mountain's sharp circle.
We are overshadowed by it, its green peak damp and fresh,
one face in the sunlight, one washed in shade.
I set out to find that place, walk across pastures
where leaves from the past settle through clouds
and mist to the kindness and beauty of rain.
This morning, the air sings with winter soon to come,
another November, another year, and life moves suddenly
away on every side. This morning, there is light in the earth
and in the stillness of words I want you to say, in the things
we have lost and the promises we kept. This morning.
Day shifts to afternoon along the edges of the far rocks.
In the quiet fields at the foot of these hills,
in the slow water of the river, the wild geese have arrived.

The Dry Season

There was no rain this summer
and the days have carried over,
one by one,
into a vast white airiness
hanging thick
between the earth and sky.

I am awake once again long before dawn,
staring up at the thin strips of the window.
There is almost nothing to see outside
from this angle, only a few dim lights
in the distance reflecting in the glass
and the high rim of trees as it traces
itself against the clouds and air.
A few last stars twinkle in a clear black sky.
A thin coating of dust gathers
in a corner of the far wall.
A small brown beetle scurries past.

I doze, then wake unexpectedly,
confused and thick-headed,
listen to her fluttering about the room,
recognize the sounds of her quick movements
as she stops here and there
the way she does every morning.
I flatten myself as far as I can,
push my face hard against the floor,
shift slightly to ease the stiff weight

of the bed's wooden slats
as they press down onto my shoulders.
The bed creaks as she sits
to pull her stockings on
and breathes a small sigh of effort
as she lifts and lowers her legs.
I lie still, breathing softly through my mouth,
stiffen in response as the mattress
presses hard against me.
I know it will lighten when she gets up.

I wonder with an inkling
of pleasure and satisfaction
if she knows that I am here.
Even if she does, I have
no plan of escape and she
will not chase me if I run.
The years here have been
acceptable to me, the unseen
participant in her routines
and exceptional events, though lately
it all seems all the more commonplace
and dull and not what I had imagined
when I first crawled that night
into this rectangular space.

Or perhaps it's because
I haven't had anything
to eat or drink all day

and the heat in this small room
grows thicker with each passing summer.

No. She is relaxed and oblivious,
accustomed to the dull sounds
of the house, lost among them
my occasional twitchings each morning
and small groans in the night.

Some days I hear the birds sing
if she opens the window
and from time to time long to feel
the air in which they live on my skin,
or want to lay myself down
in the sweet fragrance of flowers,
eyes fixed on the clouds like an old man
gazing upward consulting the spirits.

But I cannot see from here what stretches out
into a blue distance I barely remember,
try to compose myself among the dust
and lost hairpins, know it is only a matter of time
before I am discovered with a shriek
of fear or surprise or finally give myself
away at some rash and sudden hour.

It is the day I wait for:
to arise, powerful and transfigured,
and walk into the world, all light,

———

with the confidence of a deaf and blind man
who has never developed a fear
of darkness or the night.

But it is not today.

And after all, what is there to see
when you do step out
and open your eyes wide?

This morning, again, after she has left
for the secrets of life outside
that hangs in my memory
like a shapeless gray dress,
I pull my knees up to my chin,
biding my time, the white walls
around and empty bed above me
reminders of where I am,
my slow and practiced movements
on the floor in the shifting light
reassurances that I am not body but spirit
and from here can fly when I want,
inexhaustible and free,
away into the ether.

———

Spring Perspective

The water of melting snow and winter rain
in footprints alongside the house

Helpless birds in the yellow March grass

Windows cannot hold back the wind the glass
shatters you suffocate while leaning against it
in the dark room

The walls creak —
the white response
the crack in the door answering
— say
powdered earth
crumbled dust
black ash

Where does the illusion begin

All around are black flowers
red and green spores of life

How thin the moon

———

BONES

The day hangs like an old white shirt
on a rope beneath the winter trees.

In a room filled with women I move slowly,
whisper by without making a sound.
Their faces hang on a rope of light
in front of me beneath the trees.

You dream of names wet with blood
and when you wake you write *my brother*
with a sliver of bone on the walls of your room.

Thing becomes memory:
love discovered in the tiny lines around her eyes,
the corners of her mouth, the yellowness of her hair.

The thin brittle line,
winter's letters, words of ice,
the cold that binds my tongue.

*

My heart begins to pound more quickly,
I cower as if from the wind, and consider once again —
when I die, all that will remain will be clean
white bones, a dried skull, empty eye sockets
in which spiders will weave their webs,
catching everything that flies or crawls past.
That will be the penance for my sins,
fitting punishment because I wanted
to touch the moon before I died.

———

*

When I touch you, stars fall,
gather together dry and dead in your hair.

When you touch me, clouds
lift and tremble, burst into seed and flame.

Yesterday is a scattering of broken twigs
near the fence of an old house.

Today is a ragged sigh of a soul
measuring its losses in a burling wind.

Tomorrow is desire, heavy with sorrow,
a bone with wings brittle at both ends.

*

The windows of the house in which I live are painted black.
A woman I do not know stands outside all night
gathering the bones of moths from the window screens.
She tells me she believes only what her fingers can feel.
A white hole appears suddenly, a wound in the body of space.
She stretches out her hands, mouth wide, eyes closed,
wanting to touch the world beyond, offering the thin bones
she's gathered to the ghosts and gods she recognizes
and knows with every wisp of her skin and hair.

Light

Whom can you believe, what can you trust?
Forgetting is a form of loss, memory a loss of form.
Names erased so easily from a dusty black board.
I understand for a moment.
For a moment time stands still.
For a moment I remember or forget.
The house in which I live is growing cold.
Dust on my fingers.
Pain in my hands.
The white line ahead.
The black line below.
The touch of the face and belly
of the one I want to sleep with all my life.
I see her, from a distance, we talk sometimes.
Lives not shared, one body passing helpless by another.
This is how things happen, one moment at a time.
This is the time it took to get here.
I meet myself standing quietly in the dark.
I stand alongside myself, try to take my sight away.
Look. Around the corner the ineluctable light.

A Poem in Honor of Li Po

after Li Po and Tu Fu

I have forgotten my friends
my old friends
my lost friends
my dead friends
      turned to earth beneath the pines

sometimes I meet
an old man in the forest
we talk and laugh
and I forget
      to return home

let's drink more wine
I'll dance and sing
out loud
while the clear moon
      rises

THE DOOR

Light in an empty room filled with old furniture.
Careful angles and dark corners everywhere.
Each thing in its place.
The sound of distant trains, the ruts of the road.
People talking about the cold days and nights they have endured.
The transparent weeks, one after the other.
An unexpected noise in the hallway.
The clocks outside striking all at once.
Everything that was once here and important.
In the evening I don't recognize familiar colors.
The sound of love at night so close I can touch it.
The taste of discontent in all its patterns and forms.
I catch my breath, shift relentlessly, one pulse at a time.
The door will shut. The door will open.
Nothing will happen, everything will change.
Quietly carefully I make my way toward it.

IMMORTALITY

serious contemplation

of the moments

that have

just passed by

      the face in the mirror

           is my face

              and will be   my face

even if I burn it   in fire

          or

            throw myself

   off a bridge

          or into the deepest hole

rubbing   my eyes

             with my fists

    in anticipation or wakeful surprise

don't expect

     miracles

            from the body

   even I will die

        no

        I don't think so

---

my heart

                                        begins to pound

        when I think

                                        that I won't pass on

            or that I can come back

if I want   a second time

I

                am probably

                                        the only one

        I'm prepared and will not stop myself

                I know

                        that others

                                        won't like

my good fortune

                        I step back from the edge and away

                        carefully

        slowly

                                bow my head

                                touch the mirror

                                feel my face

                            _____

                                66

NOVEMBER SONG

knives

        of light

                scrape away

    the blue

            of the sky

the music of the earth

                 begins

and in my ears

       drums

             the hour

        of fear

the years will pass

      years

          without us

             without them

we will sleep a hard sleep

a pleiad

       of wild

              geese

shines

        in the heavens

listen
is it
my name

      they're singing

           as they pass by

The Solstice, Early Morning by the Window

when she left
the fingers of my right hand
webbed together - - - -

      then I could feel
      the worm's storm of lamentation
      the dreadful ocean of compassion
      the clear needle of sorrow
      the absurdly crumbling ice of love

and the snow
that misted
over everything
evenly
blindingly

in which
are born
the pains
of death's
new kingdom

the deepest
final white
point into which
the whole world
this morning descends

THE LAST WHITE BLINDING RADIANCE

when you live with prophecy
for so long
the very moment of revelation
is terrifying

the clothes
                    of old age
                                        fall
        from
                    our   bodies
                                    like
                                        dried
                                            leaves
she rises
                    lightly and easily
                                        into the sky
her face
                        not a face
                                            but
            the very expression
                                    of ecstasy
she reaches
                        the layer
                                        of clouds
        penetrates it
                        in reverse
                        evolution
                        through
                        the heart

———

                                                      of primordial
                   light
time
                            but not
                                                      eternity
          rising
                   before
                   and
                   after
                                          time
          near
                            the sudden
horizon
                                     where an unfamiliar
                                          door
                   unexpectedly
          opens
                                     and
we
                                                 stand
naked
                                          redeemed
first she
                            and behind her
                                                      I
before that
last
white
blinding
radiance

Excerpts from the Autobiography of a Man Who Casts No Shadow

it doesn't matter to me why I am
how
or
from where

I don't care about the stories of the human voice
destiny
or the daily works of God's hand
the consequences of original sin
the hypotheses of brave imagination
the security zone populated by ghosts
or you

what does it matter anyway....

I care only that my head hurts today

I look into the mirror and see nothing

I walk in the sun and cast no shadow

I stand in the doorway breathing heavily

* * *

Before getting out of bed in the morning early while it is still dark
I find and hang my bones together attach my hands and feet
finding them wherever I left them the evening before
pull on my muscles and sinews and skin

———

inside out sometimes to frighten the neighborhood's children
sew up my body's crevices and wounds with strong invisible thread
pull on the face I plan to wear that day selecting it from all the others
laid out in the dresser drawer closest to the closed closet door
push into it my forehead cheekbones and chin
fix my nose ears eyebrows lips mustache and beard insert my teeth
smooth the wrinkles on my cheeks and brow
find and combing slip on my hair in whatever color I match today
choose the appropriate underwear clothes socks shoes gloves hat
so I would nicely cover the entire form
while outside the window
above this day's head
the sun is rising
mote of dust
flake of snow
barely living thing

* * *

I found myself a wife
because I am no longer young
because I did not want my blood to die out in this world forever
because the bed creaks frozen on winter mornings
because I crawl up the stairs with empty hands
because I have begun to fear the twilights
because dusty holes gape open in all the dark corners
because the rooms have no windows
because the doors are open
- -
I wander through the house closing the doors
I hear voices everywhere speaking

———

* * *

writing my autobiography I decided to call it
Hope, Rediscovered While Stretched Out on a Freshly Made Bed
in the Stable
the first page began like this

we carry the bed outside through the door into the stable all three of us
and lift its corners onto the rafters tie them with a rope firmly
protecting it from the wind which perches hard spread-legged
on the roof howling together with the evening glow
dust rises from the sheets and pillows and settles
in the corners on the straw and spiderwebs when I lie down
it's my room the last room a special room the only room
left untouched by people and winds
not only a room but a dark passageway to the other side
where I can wander at night blindly tapping my fingers on the walls
a room without windows where closing my eyes I hear
the creaking of the wood of the house
the scratching of mice beneath the floorboards
the whistling of bird skeletons in the ridges of the roof above my head
requests for sympathy and mercy when dawn breaks
that come from nowhere and go to nowhere have no past and no future
hang quietly in yards in the neglected unhappy present
not feeding anything not seeing anything not understanding anything
awaiting their own true and final resurrection

writing that down I thought to myself do I really need this today
I turned over onto my other side and for good measure
slid down deeper under the warm sheets
I'll write the second page when I get up

---

* * *

every day in my arms or over my shoulder at the end of a stick
I carry a bag
in the bag is a box in the box is a bundle in the bundle
are a woman's ashes
mornings I sit in the kitchen waiting for the coffee to cool
holding the bag
afternoons I walk barefoot in the yard murmuring quietly to myself
touching the box
evenings when the lights go out and dogs bark somewhere far off
around the corner I stretch out on the bench
caressing the bundle
she who was turned into ash is here between my fingers but is also
a spirit let loose with the smoke into the skies
reconciled with the clouds
that's why every day in my arms or over my shoulder
at the end of a stick
I carry a bag
I know that in this way eventually I will arrange things
will create our only almost familial life together
it is pleasant to imagine
at midnight kneeling in the corner
scattering the ashes around the room
consecrating the walls and floor
I begin to laugh softly

* * *

I am the grass beneath a running child's feet
a flower that opens unseen for one day in spring
and slowly eternally closes in the evening

---

a drop of water hanging on the spider's web in the night air
a single tear on a young girl's cheek
dust of the earth pressed between primordial roots
the smell of ice and snow the touch of moon and wind
the color of the sun's song a widow's mourning dress
an unmarried woman's dozing as the day ends
a dry river filled with roosting birds
dawn's first aura evening's last flat sleep
the fog of error the mist of love
all children all parents brothers and sisters
friends relatives acquaintances lovers
philosophy dialectics music physics poetry
magic and spells war poverty misfortune hardship
applied science conscious knowledge
God's kingdom and the soul's resistance
searching the edges of the yard for its lost voice
fibers of the body and veins of wood
a drawing of the essence that explains the world
everything that can be seen or touched
matter and form
shadow
and
light
and all around
everywhere I see
everywhere my hand reaches
everything is
white
white
so white

Inscriptions in the Margins of a Prayer Book Discovered in the Eaves of an Old House After the Unnoted Death of an Unmarried Woman

o father father

I so wanted

to solve the secrets of your fingers and hair

crawl with eyes shut in the honeycombs of your bones

listen in wonder to the hymns of your nerves

swim happy and contented in the ocean of your blood

o father father

I so want

to be born a second time

return here innocent and pure

a beautiful newborn

a fortunate girl

a happy teenager

a pretty young woman

a blushing bride

a loving wife

a gentle mother

live in a fairy tale

which begins well and ends happily

in a small town

with good neighbors

a cat sleeping by the door

with geraniums beneath the windows

the sun of tolerance above my head

o father father

there is fog everywhere

the flowers are turning to dust

the fence does not protect the ground

the wind whistles endlessly in the fields

the moon sways in eternal wane

the night cuts through the distant hills

the immortal rocks gather at my feet

my hands are still empty

my eyes are growing dim

father o father

I so wanted I so want

CONFESSION

the rifle

                                      emptied

    lies

               on the floor   near

the window

he sits   leaning against the wall

            pressing into the curtain

            covering himself with a dusty cloth

in his side

                              an open

               wound

I draw near

                              kneel

             alongside

he doesn't turn his head

                                        I

                  don't know

       if he hears me

he stares at the empty wall   in front

     seeing something   in the distance

the end   of the future

        perhaps

            or

                God's

old face

        forgive me

---

   he

whispers

deep in the earth
                                     underground rivers
flow
                in dark caverns
                                 in caves
he floats on the current
                             a white flower
        in the darkness
                             dreaming of rain
he drinks its cool
drops
                  trying
                  not to give himself away
                  not to reveal
                  his infinite terrible
                  thirst
I understand
                  there's nothing   to be done
I get up
           quietly
                  like dust falling
                             on the curtains
       someone
                  whispers

                  I forgive you

My mother's mother's first lover could not have her and lay down late one summer night on the railroad tracks that ran through the fields near her father's house. They found him there the next morning, the earth gray and brown beneath him, the neighborhood's dogs trotting uneasily up and down the dirt road, the wind whistling without trace of an echo in the branches overhead.

It was a story I heard from time to time from my grandfather before he drank himself to death. He would mumble, too drained of strength to rise, in front of his wife or anyone who would listen, about how quickly his life had passed, having poured out, like the blood of that man on the tracks, in a ceaseless and unending stream. And my grandmother, with both malice and remorse, would call her husband by her lost and long-dead lover's name.

The death he chose was full of misery and shame, the indelible trace he left on my grandparents' lives as they wasted away to pain and regret, beckoned by a memory that would not fade to join him in the world beyond.

I remembered all three of them when I stood on those tracks in the middle of those fields near the remains of my great-grandfather's house, understanding how even those who perish in obscurity, half a world away, leave their marks on the faces of those at night who close their eyes and listen to the silence after the trains in the distance have passed by.

He died before my children were born and I tell them about him
sometimes, when I tell our family's stories – uncle and godfather, raw-
boned and visionary, alcoholic son and failed father, in the end a weak
reed no one leaned upon, who struggled with his gloom and self-
loathing and was caught in a trap he laid for himself in the teeth of the
wind.

He would listen to me in moments of clarity, drawing a breath
as if wanting to speak and then letting it out in a sigh and waiting for
me to talk myself out. He would nod when I said that life is not
something that was waiting for us around the corner but was here and
now, and then would ask me for money for a bottle of sweet wine, too
tired and shaky to invent another lie. It was not for his thirst, he would
say, but because with it everything grew remote and the stars in the
sky began to swim and the horizon expanded again.

Once he said he thought we gave birth to our death, like
something lifting inside us, like the tunnel where he thrashed and
choked and could not breathe because there was no light. That's how
they found him early one morning as the sun touched the edges of his
room: the artery in his liver spilling his life out into something scarlet
and black, his nose burrowed between the thighs of the woman he
lived with like a small lost dog looking for the place he'd come from
and where he wanted to return.

I think of him like that but do not tell my children the details of
his final story: lying in the dark in a pool of his own blood, not
knowing what was rolling over him as a veil of grayness covered his
eyes, perhaps dreaming one last time of the daughter he had
abandoned or the grandchildren he would never see or the angels that
would come to him with the wine in the dead of night.

It was not until years later, until we remembered the things he had said, that we could begin to understand the reach and measure of his death.

He said he had stood on ground where no sun had ever shined, behind a door that opened onto a night that was impenetrably black.

He said that shadows sprouted around him like dark flowers watered by the rain that fell only on barren soil.

He said that something inside him had gone or was letting go, like a curl of smoke dissolving in the sky or a whirlwind roaring in the utter silence that shaped the deepest truths that were the blight on the heart of his family and his life.

He said he had groped forlornly inside his head, searching for the tunnel that would lead him out and away while the whole world spun around him like the chamber of his father's gun.

The sound of his death was the flat concussion of a bullet exploding in the spinning chamber of his father's gun, the link to the past and future he held clenched when they found him in his stiffening hand.

His bones are turning white in a place where his father has never been but knows how to find.

———

Rhapsody

We sit on hard wooden chairs in front of a small raised stage on which a man sits on a wooden chair in front of us. He is dressed in a white shirt and dark pants illuminated by a harsh flat light that casts no shadow.

We watch him, with no sense of concern or alarm, as he begins to burn.

We have been here before and know it is a question of who can endure this the longest: we who sit in front of him or he who sits in front of us, he who burns or we who watch him burn.

We know it is a question of how long we would be content to watch.

Until all that he is peels from his bones?

Until the blood no longer beats as loud in our ears with each new wooden chair arranged and illuminated on each small stage?

Until the last such spectacle ends in truth and resurrection?

He would not move when the flames began, saying the moment was his triumph and destiny, and later could not.

The first dull moan of pain finds its way from his throat, the sound of what was once a man now broken and lost.

Some around me clap and stomp their feet, some whistle and laugh.

Somehow I find myself tangled in white sheets lying at the feet of a man with sores on his arms. The echo of a thin moan circles the frayed edges of his body and gathers in the wisps of his hair. His hand reaches for me and I roll my arm up in a corner of the sheet and stretch it forward, afraid to touch his skin. The bones of his hand rub through the cloth and grate against me and I am wracked in dry revulsion.

I stand in the tub washing myself, scrubbing away the touch of that skin and bone, chafing my flesh until blood begins to appear in pinpricks on my legs and arms. I tremble in long ripples.

He lies in bed and seems to be sleeping, a long white bundle with one eye rolled back. I feel my heart grow heavy.

Clean and washed free of the touch I recall half in memory and half in imagination, I wait for the tremors in the bed on the other side of the room to subside. I eat and sleep and am at last content.

I breathe fast and shallow, my belly and arms pocked by sores and small scabs. Somehow I am dressed in his clothes and lie tangled in white sheets and moan softly as someone I do not know stares up at me from the foot of the bed. I stretch my hand out to touch him.

THE RIVER

The sky is pure white and the air is still. The dogs drag back and forth across the grass, whining with eagerness, kicking up tufts of earth clinging to old roots. The bodies of the rabbits are lined up neatly in rows on a flat slab of thin metal, marks made by dirt and the work of the dogs distinguishing one from the other. I dig a hole on the banks of the river, shaping a shallow pit in which to bury the rabbits, forming small neat piles of earth in a circle around it. When the hole is made, I pick up the slab on which the rabbits lie and walk slowly back to the hole, kicking up the dust and tasting the smell of the soil. One of the rabbits falls off the metal slab and kicks its hind leg straight out unexpectedly. It lies crumpled and abandoned on the ground, moving in fits and starts. My heart quickens as I watch it. I find myself in a pocket of air in which time stands still. I bend down and lift the rabbit up by the loose skin of its back and press it close to my chest as I grasp its head in my right hand and snap its neck. Its spine will not flex and breaks just above the shoulders. The pocket of air and time in which I stand fills with the dense smell of the rabbit as I carry it back to the metal tray. The flies are there before me, rising in a cloud from the rows of furred bodies and buzzing impatiently as I wave my arms above them. They will not follow these creatures into the hole I've dug along the riverbed. When they are buried, I will live alone again, awaiting a similar extinction. In the years to come, when the river rises and roars up in flood, perhaps it will wash over all of us buried on these banks and mix our bones together.

85

The cricket under the table in the kitchen tells a story in a language I have never heard, with a voice muffled as the cry of someone in the desert drowned in sand and loud as the tumbling of dust. It is a story about odd creatures who slide away into the night, who hiss and rattle in vengeance and threat under rocks and dead holes, who form the core of a universe of predators in the world's hidden corners and great flat plains. The cricket tells the story with a conviction so intense that its voice is thick with admiration and wonder for the things it cannot understand and yet describes. It is like a ceremonial of cleansing, a numbering of visions and signs, a chanting of the beliefs of generations forged anew each night in this retelling beneath the dull dark sky. I find it here in the early hours of the morning, a comfort when I am unable to sleep, the story it repeats continuously as much a part of this room as my breathing. I know that all stories end, that the hours pass in this land and that one and in all the rest of the world. I face that fact more frequently now and it is no longer a moment of astonishment or pain. When the time comes, I want to die in my bed, in a familiar place, and be mourned by my children and old friends. The cricket understands this, accepts me into the weaving it makes of its answers and truths, and I am borne up like a scrap of paper on the wind and then sink back calm and free into the dark river of its words.

THE WORD

The word she hurled at me in the kitchen was a nail driven through my
hand into the polished wood of the table. I can no longer leave this
small room. I accept the limitations of my destiny, express no regrets,
voice no complaints. I fix my gaze on the glass of the window, watch
the whole scene repeat itself as the light outside changes to the color
of gray rags. She tries to pull it out each night as I sleep bent across
the table, but the nail holds, it holds.

Our son would have been photographed in a garden, among the fruits and blossoming flowers, light streaming evenly across the sky, his face luminous with curiosity, his bright eyes a reflection of the deepest desire I am capable of. Our son would have been photographed in a garden, running to you at the edge of the yard as a soft breeze stirred the leaves and caught and lifted the hem of your summer dress. Our son would have been photographed in a garden, and the pictures we would have kept in albums and desk drawers would surprise us when we found them and we would say then that this is how life should be.

Year after year the garden pours forth its seeds, resurrecting itself, and the things that grow here are tended with love. As I make my way among them, I am comforted and at last content to know that our son would have been photographed with you in a garden.

Epiphany

I once believed there is nothing worse than what we can imagine: the body stiff with solitude, the face blank and featureless and little more than a rapid bulge under the skin, the soul an old parcel of eggs hidden in a deep dark corner of an abandoned barn. The protection of imagining the worst has not protected us. There is a time and place for everything, and today, quite unexpectedly, the worst is here.

All these passing moments, all the ephemeral things of the world, and now, suddenly, something I can embrace and keep as if forever: the tiny white-bellied bird on the red flower swaying in the wind near the green and silver waters of the sea in Mayagüez!

The light is out and the air is heavy with the smell of burned candles. The moon is dark and the night outside is still, though from time to time the wind rattles the windows and doors to a sound like the crackling of gravel. In the hour before dawn, the coldest hour, I unroll a long white cord to mark off the place where I will spend the remainder of the day, moving backwards slowly on my hands and knees across the floor, feeling my way from corner to corner as the sides of my body rub against and trace the dim shapes of things that have not been dusted for a long time, faint blurs in the blackness of the mirrors and windows surrounded by the strands of the woven cord.

Laying the square requires patience and meticulous resolve. Although I try to set them right, the corners into which the cord unfolds itself have different shapes each time I call them into being and the line, which stretches out from my hands to the dimensions of an uncertain expanse, to the four endpoints of the only space I can claim as my own, an earth I understand, can crumble at the slightest touch, dissolve in the briefest moment, transfigure from discipline and geometric order to the chaos of the deepest recesses in the darkest hole. And so I take my time to shape this line of cord, forge these four corners, invent this emerging square, beyond the reach of philosophy or law, groping my way through a place that grows less manifest each day, wanting to keep from becoming the kind of spectacle or luminous display that corrupts the hearts of the innocent and young.

I am especially careful today, more of a ghost of myself than ever, understanding with the power of everything I am and feel that every premonition of disaster can be confirmed or denied, though I know too that there is no consolation or solace in such knowledge.

Sometimes I think I am approaching the point at which the corridors I fashion within my square of shifting corners may lead nowhere and that the foundations I build of unwinding cord are the obscure traces of a history lost or long forgotten that I mimic and fulfill. If this is true, I do not mind and it does not matter. I stretch the cord into the corners of its square and take my place inside it. As the wind breaches the walls of the room and builds to blowing sand and crack of gravel, I turn my back and dream of night and endure.

First Light

It was the things they sang about that caught my attention as I opened my eyes that day for the first time:

a face full of earth, deep, impenetrable, restless, in a room encrusted with beetles and dirt;

toads croaking unexpectedly in the enormous silence of solitude and cold;

a dog howling as winter startles the dry leaves and uproots the delicate heads of flowers from the hard rock of the ground in tiny gray bits and pieces;

the roll of muffled drums trembling in the silence of the frozen battlefields, the night banging against its own stars;

a bird, flying low across the line of the horizon, suddenly erased by snow and wind.

All these things, after a sleepless night broken by the fall of dawn as it emerges from obscure corners, and the same voices this morning that persist in my ear.

The Sound

The sound that rounds the corner is dry and brittle as old wood. The dead who lived here are long dead, having passed through the gates of their bones like vapor, having lifted away from the flesh that love transfigures to mystery and sorrow with empty hands. The sound rounding the corner is the clothing that memories and fears are made of, elusive as a wisp of smoke, ineffectual as the flicker of hope in the hearts of prisoners perched on the brink of the ditch into which their bodies will fall. The sound is the snare of longing and regret, the descent into the sleep of wingless creatures that toss through the night with one eye open and rise despirited and haggard at the coming of dawn. It is a message that never changes, and as I listen I don't know who else can hear.

THE LACE MAKER

These pictures of solitary women in light-filled rooms, allegories of faith and innocent desire, soft brooding moments filtered through leaded glass, the dissolved contours in variegated perspective and composed balance — all purity and harmony, the blurred strands of red and white thread that fall onto the lace maker's table, her face consecrated with the sanctity of simple pleasures as if life itself was gathering up to embrace her, the significance of ordinary things, simple actions treasured as divine gifts, and the light enters her and she draws breath again, the breath of truth, obligation, and piety, and in Vermeer's hands when she is gone this is her life, waiting for the passage that grows no darker as the days pass, never moving from that fixed scene to mystery or transcendence, her soul showing through the flesh, beyond the farthest void, the distillation and fate of her love, the deep down stirring of the knowledge a woman alone has.

I think of her when I lie in bed at night and stare into the dark hole into which I am falling. I wonder if she is an angel come to show me the way out. She goes before and I follow, my eyes shut in order to see.

Like all gardeners, I am bound to the patch of dirt I cultivate and to the seeds I plant, each a universe of labor and each a point in the tally of the passing days. In the cleared ground are the remains of neatly tended vegetables and flowers. The last few tomatoes on the vines in the small plot of garden alongside are very small and deeply red. Their leaves are already furling and drooping and the creepers that shoot out across the ground wind toward the grass beyond the fence and wither slowly in the cold dry air.

I come here without fail every day, even in the fading late afternoon light of this closing season, to clear and turn the soil, to make sure the earth does not grow too hard to tend as the nights grow colder, as the wind reminds us that work here for the year is nearly done. Time bears everything onward and forward in its flow and there is in fact now little left to do, only to gather stray leaves from time to time and turn them over into the earth, listen to the silence that drops across the garden when the wind in the trees unexpectedly stops, record the changes of the moon.

It is possible in this way to be both body and spirit, to know that there will be another summer in which to try again, another time to be sure the seed does not die out.

VERMONT MORNING

A pale light, cool and dry, seeps through the walls and door. Rain washes the mist that feeds on stones, prunes trees to cudgels of brown and green. Clusters of stars dissolve to shadows thin as paper at the wood's edge and unfold from ridge to ridge like the slow pulsations of silence and time.

I remember the shape of the sky along the curved bank of trees above the drifting of foxglove and bluet, the wooded crests of the hills trembling with clouds, muddy boards by the barn, a thrush singing, the smell of the soil after that April rain, the frail sun huddled above the surface of the pond lighting the delicate bend in the wall of piled stones, the curtained windows, the gentle swell of her breasts.

As I wake from sleep in the spring in the darkened room layered by light that seeps in crescents through the walls and door, the rain downwind, skimming the moss on the cedar roof of the barn near the maze of pastures, speckling the wild rose that flowers pale each summer against the morning sky, smoky as the distant hills, as I wake from sleep without her, I suddenly remember.

My eye is a flower shut tight at the center of a closed circle. I sit on the bus by the window beside a woman who smells like falling rain. She talks quietly. I hear the landscape of rain, the hiss of lamps on street corners dimmed by rain, the chiming of bells and dreams of glory, the melody of expectation and promise – full of movements and pauses – enlivened and animated by rain. My eye is an insect on her lithe, white thigh. As it moves, I know that I know women and how women are like rain.

She could not use the gift of prophecy she was born with and closed
her eyes for hours on end, waking up suddenly from one formless
dream or another stiff and cold, a human spirit beyond call or
classification, the last of her kind.

It was wasted, she said, on someone like her, who lived in a
place where words could not enter, having coiled away in inconsistent
directions and from which the visions she monitored could not
emerge.

It was there, she said, that she defended the world against the
beasts that stared from under dead roots and out of holes, forming
their bizarre shapes into answers to the questions she deciphered
among the gestures of expiation and the genuflections made by those
around her as darkness fell.

She hears them, turning in the direction
of a sudden noise, a steady building roar
in which no single sound can be
distinguished, the stuttered revelations
of ecstatic souls.

She keeps her eye fixed on the gates,
hearing nothing but what goes on inside
her, wrapped up in the pulsing of her
blood, watching for the figures that
come through unexpectedly from the
farthest void.

She lives a life unmediated by words,

apart from the quarreling of voices,
outside the dominion of ideas,
omniscient as dry bones held together
by dust and cobwebs in the urgent
present of the eternal moment.

She understands that the truths we know
lie in inessential acts, in the silences
between us, yet she fails to see the moment
at which together they wax and wane.

I have not seen the ghosts in this house but have felt them touch me
from time to time, emerging from between the walls in various rooms
and brushing my back lightly with the tips of their fingers, like a
stirring of air on my skin moved by the flicker of brittle wings. The
first time, I turned with a start, a cornered, uncertain look in my eyes,
thinking there was someone else unexpectedly with me in the house,
feeling suddenly cold; the second not remembering what I had
planned to say if it happened again, the thought eluding me like a wisp
of smoke in the wind; and each time after feeling the first stirrings of
welcome for whatever would come to put an end to thought and
dream, for the moment when the door clicks softly shut and the ghosts
move slowly through the house to put together the pieces this life has
disarranged.

    I often write in the kitchen, alone late at night, hunched over
the table with a single hanging lamp above my head shining down on
the paper and glinting, as it moves almost imperceptibly back and
forth, on the ink as it dries. I lay out the pieces of those pieces,
emerging translucent and blind from the recesses of the page like the
ghost who stands behind me whispering in my ear. I write because the
absent are present when we think of them, groping in memory for a
grief past weeping, for a bridge however makeshift or temporary
across the silence that has fallen between us in the passing years.
Sometimes when the words don't come and something still presses,
nudges inside me, I look up from the page and down the hall at the
chair standing alone in the dimly-lighted room at the opposite end, and
see myself there, sitting quietly at first and then suddenly dodging
from shadow to shadow, ready to climb up and into the darkest corner
of the farthest wall. Something happens then, though it is different

every time, slow, mysterious, and dense, and I stare fascinated and afraid, reaching out from inside the wall to touch the next one in the house who passes by.

But the hour is late and no one comes and once again I struggle to climb down on my own out of the corner of this wall, find my way along the hall back to the table in the kitchen. Time is short and the question here is always the same: who are the ghosts and who are the presences in our lives; who is inside the wall bursting to get out and who leans against it, bending it in?

PRIAM'S DAUGHTER

I. *Touching the Moon*

A slice of light, half-curled above
the tree line, settled to smoky threads
along the horizon as night dimpled
snow in the dark fields and the creek's
cold edges thickened to a polished spill
the color of old birches. After dark,
the wind right and pines hovering
close to the ground, clouds rubbed
against a cut of stars that slipped
in a darkening slide to a clearing
half-lost in the mountains. It was a place
where dark flowers grow and cicadas grate
in solitude and vacancy, the sound
of their strumming suspended
like dust in the faint light that draped
the faded edges of the sky. She found
that place alone, listening to the wind,
as we quivered among the noises
of that starlit night and watched her
climbing over shadows that lay
like dark bruises on the season-plowed soil.
She climbed to touch the moon,
to break the trance of the nightfall
that surrounded her, push through
the cold clouds that curled north on the wind
where the hill ascends and reclaim
the emptiness she said was ours.

We were all divining life in those
dark corners then, skirting
its dangerous edges, each stirred
by a different pulse of the wind.
Caught there like a sift of leaves
against the tree line, we did not want
to understand when she said that nothing
lay beyond the things she feared
and lived by, that morning
always came to her in a heaving
under clear sheets of water,
that hollow trunks of trees
are warm as blood and their dark wood
opens to seed beds where the year's dead
are transfigured by the moon
and skim the earth like feeder roots
pulled loose from the lost ground below.
We watched her, in a dream
without sleep, waiting for a signal,
a wisp of smoke or quiet tapping of stone
to pierce the shadows. Her face was
as disconsolate as the moon she reached for
and all around gaped open burrows
where small animals slept, their soft skins
hardening white in the unaccustomed thudding
and jostling of the night air. Its odd light
seeped to our marrow and we moved
toward that place with arms extended,
drifting past each other like dark footfalls
in empty passageways before stumbling

104

into silence. The patterns in the sky
unexpectedly changed and she was
suddenly gone, a rustling of birds
in the veerings of the wind.
Although we had come to sink with her
into a nuzzling of thorns
in the gray scrub bushes, there
was nothing else we could see
in that place, only clouds and trees
awash in a dark green light
that dissolved to an abstract of angles
and lines on the water. The chill
in the wind smoldered in the darkness
and the hours before dawn opened slowly,
like the shell of a dying newborn bird.
In that light, traced like panic against
the paling sky, we knew she was gone,
a scuttle of mist thickening to the cool dark
of the earth, a quick return to dust,
and we were left alone with the moon
hanging black against the stars,
silent and forbidding, and the sound of the wind
whistling endlessly across the hills.

II. *The Nightingale's Song*

The air tasted of metal and the sky
was passionless as glass. In that slow
realization of light, as clouds
unraveled the fine dust and swept lines
of the moon above my head, I stretched out
my hands and the frozen flowers
in the meadows blossomed, rainbows
in the trees' hanging branches
glowed with the bodies of fragile butterflies,
time drifted like moonrise across wet ice
in a spark and warp of heady smoke.
Wait! I can hear them. But I don't think
they pity us. We blend to sorrow and strife
in the wounds and leavings of new birth,
and hunger advances in the wild hour,
and I wait here for my breath to settle,
for the fear to go away as the nagging surge
of needled hearts startled in every direction
probes like braided wire for the parch and peel
of blood. I lay for a long time near the stumps
of the yellowing pines, a patch of fallen white
against the fading green, bristling in flutters
and shivers, and heard their voices
pulling my bones this way and that,
whistling in the caverns behind my eyes
like the climax of some unspeakable hour.
They could not hear me when I cried
that this dream was not enough,

106

the work of the spirit falling to elegy and ruin,
the way back a lost moment hammered
in secrecy hard as steel in the forge of night.
I am blocked whatever way I turn, in cough
and blind panic. And I know there is nothing
beyond the things I've feared and lived by,
nothing they could find or name, only the darting hiss
and click of the moon's pale blood, slow hunger
stinging eyes fixed on the grass, stamens
veined and coiling. They don't believe me,
bloodless and apologetic, though all my life
I've named that weariness of the heart
that scatters quickly into the night like dry leaves,
building patterns that long for extinction,
a hundred gray shapes that pass among the trees
like a tide of blind mouths flying off to oblivion.
Root clenching root, blending to hard earth,
the hypothesis of dark desires,
and the life that moved within me
silent now and thick-fingered as roots
sprouting from clods and dead holes
stretched and laboring forward, sinews oiled,
tasting stone. I know they didn't pity me
even as the years passed across
the dry-veined sky and clotted hard
among the oaks and pines and lines
of cedar angled thin in the snow.
They don't remember that now
or understand why I need the moon's
pure light above me, high in the hills,

a vacuum into which everything collapses,
stripped to the numbness of bone.
I cannot reach it. I cannot reach it.
Listen! Do you understand I am not
this empty space that splinters to light,
the womb of earth, infinity's blind shore?
I climb only to touch the moon, to reclaim
the thing that once was mine, afraid
that my story has already had its end. Deeper
than the eye can follow, its pale light stiffens
in the mist, plain, placid and clear, and trails off
forever in a welter of silver that glowers
and pierces every shadow. I've heard them say it,
and in my deepest heart I know it's true.
My life is sprung bone, dull with reluctance,
longing to be filled in a world in which nothing fills.
And so it begins. I can hear them behind me,
voices borne on the wind at night
in a rustling of birds. The moon is up,
a halo of clarity that thins and thickens
and is sucked out again into the dark
like the ghosts that vanish as I touch them.

THE METAPHYSICS OF WOLVES

1.

The old woman rides the wolf
through the grained scarlets
of the sinking sky.
Wind licks her face,
thrust to a clouded howl,
and her blind eyes rest
on nothing, tongue stretched
in a scratching lurch
to the dark and shearing
blood of night.

2.

No protection, nothing
to keep the blur of wind
from tearing at our bones.
We cross packs of ice
hard and dark as a clot
of blood, backs arched
to knives of fear: ahead
a ragged line of skittered
shadows hunches fanged
in the cut of the field.

3.

Slices of shadow stalk
the sun, withering
in the fraying light
that pulps the weeds to dust.
We leap with the wolves
through the driven grass,
tethered jaws stretched
tight as wire, and string
them up like hunted birds
on the crisp and shredded air.

4.

Bones, wolf bones, shafts
of fire sparking
in the soil, steaming
in the hard beaten rain,
the long sift of ash
coiled in the darkening rain,
the swift bones sawing
through the soil, burned
to white stone in the quaver
and pump of silting rain.

5.

Morning chars the green
and pitted sky,
crumbling to white spines
that crackle like broken glass
under the skin of the red moon.
These things are fibered
vapor: the wolves still stir
in the bone yard, cusped between
their frozen dead and wailing
low in the wind and flame.

6.

There is nothing left to fear,
only thin bands in the sky that strobe
toward a foam of clouds leeching
the new moon, stars sprawled and brittle
as old bones, broken shadows sputtering
like flocks of wolves across the dark grass.
Do you hear them? Those howls,
hurled from nowhere to nowhere,
are the despair of another season
ground to powder under our heels.

7.

Those were the signs
we watched for, in that time
of pity and addled hope, things
that can be named like blood
in the cheeks or marks on bare wood
clawed to a lace work of exhaustion
and sorrow that smothers
the air. The rapture of self
in the shells of these creatures,
the sound of wind in an empty place.

8.

Nothing is plain, stirred
by the gesture of an unseen hand,
discouraged and cold as the dead
no one comes to remember
when the wolf moon rises, sheer
and gray as a shiver of recognition,
beyond the fullness of care and neglect
and the lost reasons of our lives.
Its light tonight is all
that makes the world persist.

9.

The sky clears to a dead bolt
of gray and the promise
of snow cracks like a dry branch
in the wind. The first stars
are out, streaks and pulses
and whorls of light that bite
into the earth. Ah God!
The turmoil of marrow, the singing
of nerves, the bellow of terror
from the depths of our lungs.

10.

The silence of the day falls away
to the low sound of God's name
in the hiss of memory
and old confusions, harnessed
to the shudder of the changing air,
stutter in the redemption of wind
and inwardness of stone.
Listen! The wolves whisper
of life to come quickened
in the depths of profoundest night.

St. Francis at Alverna

1.

The bells swing back and forth in the gray towers
and the town's deaf mutes collapse in the streets.
They are burning the last remnants of this plague.
The eyes of the bodies in the market place
are the color of ochre and melted wax
and take their nourishment from the passing air.
Blackened bandages flutter like banners in the wind.
I spin my trail from door to door roaming blank
across their field of vision, patient and bloodless,
crying out for forgiveness and redemption.
No one answers. It is the same everywhere,
the seeds of the thorn bush that sprouts in the graveyard.
My voice hangs still and vacant as an echo
above the smoldering flames and the dust rising
for the day of resurrection that will never come.

2.

The man with no hands weaves
the day from motes of dust and shadow.
Hovers on wings carved from tree roots.
Speaks but does not answer.
Stands wedded to the impotent stars.
Works quickly, without assistance,
pierced by perfidy and forgetfulness.
Knows which things conceal
the contours of being.

Does not know who I am.
Does not know himself
or the name of God
in the uneasy rasping
of this final hour.

3.

The perfected lie the word that drones
and drones inside my head the clever
madness in this time of confusion and faith
common signs in the limp of night
fixed to allegories of balked desires
uneasy consciousness of absences and gaps
in the pale smoke of each other's signals
the empty shell of language rattling
with the dried peas of forgotten words
the pronouns of intimacy
from the first letter to the last
the mystical contemplation
of the incarnate word
the maze that defines
the monologue of the self
as it swells with envy
in the babble of its cell
all this —

I haunt the streets like distant whistling
I cannot stretch my hand out to stop

4.

The announcement was distorted
by an incidental emotion.
No one listens to the explanation.
I call near the window:
Pay attention!
Remember these signs and blood!
The voice caught in the wind answers:
the scar has whitened,
the stigmatic mark.
Amid the grate of bone
and sift of skin to dust
the blind spot hurtles
into the maw of the future.

Maine Aubade

1.

The simple lyrics of waves
and sea flowers stutter
like feathery tufts of light
through darkness brittle
as charred paper. Loose shapes
of birds clip the water,
trolling the banks
of the Kennebunk, and slip
without sound through reeds
pared by the stitch of night.
On this narrow furrow
of shore wedged between
the river and sea, you touch
your fingers to my wrist,
in one cupped hand holding
the pale shells you gathered
to catch the light. The grasses
creak and the moon casts
small circles on the river,
spiking white slivers of water
that hum with the cold
flat voice of the wind.

2.

The tuned gathering of mist
and clouds above water
that cannot hold the tympanic moon
shrouds the horizon like gray gauze.
Waves in the distance break
in a noiseless slide, lines
smoothed to sheets of dark green
oiled by dapples of light
from shore that flash
off the contours of watery foam
ruffled by a wind far out at sea.
Quickened tangles of birches
and scrub pines press forward
in half-relief toward sand
leached to blue shadows
by the curl of the coming tide.
Head down, you stare into the fire
as it reddens the stacked
driftwood and lights your hair,
flames fingering the leaves
of the trees that frame you and moving
like brittle chimes in the wind.

3.

The landscape is suddenly still
as the cramped angle and thin
crack of sky shift blue
along the bend in the river
and flatten to a wedge of yellow
that threads with the current
among the knobbed rocks,
sliding back upon itself
and retreating into shadows
bent as sticks in clear water.
In this place preserved from the sea,
under the worn fingers of trees
thinning to clouds and fog
above the river, you trace
the outline of the dead bird
lit by the moon in the sand,
wing feathers gray as stone,
hissing like the wind hollowed
at dead center, like sagging leaves
fluttering against the scrape of water,
like unmoored things drifting
aimless and shimmering to silence.

4.

The veiled flanks of the river
are flecked with primrose and laurel,
flowers gone to the hard mercy
of wind that skims shoals
thick and black with mussels. The bristle
of water in eddies and pools
thickens an octave to a soft lament
trembling among rocks sour
with the sea's smell curling
in the measured breeze from the east
that brings the first taste of dawn
to birds unwound on the shifting waves.
You stretch strands of eelgrass
across the rocks, arrange pieces
of driftwood softened by water
like a cradle or trap around the tide
pool at your feet, foraging in water
streaked by first light for signs
of life, face pressed against knees
that muffle a voice rising slowly
from your hollows like a small cry
lost between the sea and wind.

———————

5.

Water spreads luminous and thin
across the pale blue bruise
of morning as it shifts to white
in the pulse of reeds ringed
by the crouch of night. The play
of light bursts among the twisted vines
where the sea and river turn to land
and the sting of water hardens
to circles of dark birds strumming
the trees, the shape of something
fragile and small scattered to flight,
trickling through crevices of fog
in the clustered shallows
that mark the end of the season.
Forgotten like a seed cast
on dry sand, your face softens
to a weightless blur mitered
in the scrim of morning by bird song
that floats like mist across the inlet
where water brushes the sky
and touches us, transfigured by light
to counterpoints of silence and wind.

Seeing Wyeth's *McVey's Barn* Seventeen Years Later

In this place of memory
beneath a sky full of branches
ringed by the far-off hum
of cicadas, light powders
the quiet weave and dust
of straw. Shadows sprinkled
across the coarse boards
crumble like braids of dirt
tapped from dry roots.
A touch of pale color,
like shadings of brush stroke
or line, trembles above
the sleigh burrowed high
on the brown rafters, spreads
in the still afternoon air
like gray smoke, rising and
fading in the loose darkness
of this New England barn.

Small birds gather in the grass
and the blue jay's song lifts
across the narrow yard.
Your footsteps still echo
on these floorboards where we
danced naked that summer
thinking no one would see,
our bodies dusted with light
that filtered through the thin

barn walls with the sweet
smell of late roses. And though
half our lives have passed,
that afternoon has not left
this place, locked in the warm
smells of barn straw and flowers
and dappling the walls like
bird song or pale dust washed
by a haze of fragile light.

INHERITANCE

In his last days, my grandfather
would tell me to search the sky
for omens in the waning hours
of night, for clouds the shape
of crosses portending war, dispersions
of stars swept like white dust
behind the darkest corner of the moon
auguring illness and death, streaks
of light, oranges and bloody reds,
divining the smoldering contours
of famine in the hours before dawn.

Now, whenever the wind trembles
the house and the clouds
are odd angles black against
the paling sky, I stumble
suddenly from sleep and reach
to open the window, watching
the horizon for signaled changes,
pushing back in absence to the dark
of the room to wait for the whistling
of the wind to stop, the dry echo
of my grandfather's voice in my ear.

FREIGHT TRAINS

for my brothers

There is something reassuring even now
in the sound of a passing train
lifting in the night wind and settling
with the rain against the corners
of the house. It fills the room,
and I remember how still we would lie
late into night in the old green house
on Millard's hill listening for trains
as rain tapped soft and gray across
the latticed shadows of the porch roof.

The freight cars would roll with the clouds
in the distance by Schultz's field, sliding
through the late summer air and whistling sweetly
in towns they passed to up the road.
We found comfort in that, without knowing
where they were going or where they had been,
as if we had found a place screened
from the wind in the dark trees or shaped
by the colors of night as they soften
the edges of things outside the open window.

On those nights now when my children
whisper tenderly in their sleep and I lie
in bed as the wind rises and wanes
listening to freight trains in the distance

---

roll north up from the yards in New Haven,
I remember you there, so quiet and close,
watching the stars in the trees drift
toward dawn like the lights of summer
that passed the bottom of the hill, their names
the first and last sounds on our journey.

MY FATHER'S WINE

after Vytautas P. Bložė

My father made wine
and buried it in large bottles
in the orchard soil
and year after year
the wine fermented
among the roots of apple
trees and cherries.
And then he was gone,
taken by them
that spring
with a knock on the door
in the dead of night,
buried far away
by an unnamed road
at the forest's edge.
He could not find his wine
beneath the ground
where they put him.
They would not let us
look for it among
the orchard's roots
and I never felt
its sweetness on my tongue.
But I know
that when we are all together
in the ground
and the light of memory

has changed to something
deep and clear,
we will gather around him
to drink that homemade wine.
My father will lift
the first glass
to all our living and dead,
and the absence
that was ours will touch
and shape that moment
with its sweet last sound,
and our deep thirst
will quicken our resolve
and our desires.
And I know that mine
will be the first head
to spin and that I
will be the first to cry,
to cry that while alive
I never had the chance
to taste my father's wine.

FEBRUARY SNOW

It is snowing again tonight
and the sounds of the bells
from the church on the Green
whisper low around
the corners of New Haven.
Light from the street lamps
ruffles through the windows,
silver blue in the snow
that sifts endlessly
in the cool green pines
that border the yard.
Here inside this small white house
where my daughters sleep,
I walk in the dark
with a familiar creak
of floorboards, checking the doors,
drifting slowly past the windows,
each step framed
by that thin-veined light
that comes from the north
with the snow
on silent February nights.
There are memories in it,
of other snowfalls and other houses,
the odd comforts of darker days
now as silent as the stars
that slip away to clouds bearing snow,
a certain melancholy knowledge

---

of beginnings and endings,
old friends gone, the years
passing as unexpectedly
as the storm's frail sounds
suddenly whisked away
from the house by the wind
toward the harbor.
But there is still this night
and this snow and the quiet
breathing of my children.
Downstairs, the wood stove
is filled with embers
and purling, the fire settling
to ashes on the cold grate.

Raking

In late July, as evening wreathes
the red maple and clouds pass
east thick with orange light,
we rake tiny apples from the grass
that still lies flat with the afternoon's heat,
gathering the hard green fruit
the trees have dropped and rolled
to the small far corners of the yard.
The weight of their branches brings
them close, smelling of summer,
sweet with the rich tastes
of the season that petal the air.

My daughters help with the raking,
playing with the apples piled
in the wooden basket in a weave
of grasses and twigs tangled
as a bird's nest, their faces,
turning every few minutes to watch me,
bright and warm in circles of light
filtering through the midsummer leaves.

And as they played, I raked up
the body of a young bird,
neck folded awkwardly back
against its stiff wings, from beneath
the white pine I planted
in the spring. It was hard

---

and the color of the ground
and I took it over to the basket,
calling my children away, to lay it
like a spotted apple among
all the other living things
the trees had dropped this year.

And as I placed it in the basket
among the twigs and grasses,
I remembered an earlier season
and another bird, my parents readying
the garden for spring, rakes clicking
against fallen branches, and my sister
catching a robin with
a broken wing under a wooden basket

and how the bird fluttered and died
without a sound late that afternoon
when I brought it pieces of apples
and bread to eat and pushed the edge
of the lifted basket down against
its back, trying to keep it safe
from the things of night when it tried
to hop away, and how birds since then
sing in my sleep, their midnight cries
thick with a sense of death
that awakens to whistles of forgiveness
in the pausings of the wind.

My daughters don't understand
why I tell them to keep away
but will not come closer, as if they know
with some hidden childhood sense
that there are secrets none of us
should know revealed by the things
that lay tangled together in the basket
they have made their plaything.

And though I sometimes find it hard
to say, I know I want to keep them
from the muffled cries and flutterings
of creatures that die in innocence,
the quick turn toward that other light,
the singing in sleep that shapes
the shadows of things gone long before
we would give them up. So in this
raked garden, thirty years later,
I widen the circle, in my children's play
among the dropped apples trying to find
and preserve whatever it is I lost.

LOVE

after Miroslav Holub

Two thousand cigarettes.
A hundred miles
from wall to wall.
Our lives a vigil
for something whiter
than snow.

Now, words are dry,
like seagull footprints
in the sand,
sweepings, dust.

Bitter, you say,
the world's beginning.
You laugh when I say
how beautiful it was.

NORTH LIGHT

1.

The wind changes, stirring the gray of early morning.
In the old November garden lie blackthorn, seed, and spore,
shadows and bird bones in the brittle north light.

The flecked glow of ice on dry grass, the fingers of cloud
against the sky, the salt veins of stones, the deepest roots
in dry weather, in the bursting and cudgeling light.

2.

There is something beyond and perishing, crackling
in the bark of the oak and poplar. A cry lost on the wind.
An old dream of beginnings and endings in the deepening light.

Things hard and alive. The silence of beating wings.
The rocks dark and singing. The sigh and shiver
of wind where the water meets the north light.

3.

The silence of forgotten things knocks like the wind
against the moon in November. Branches in the garden
washed white by the rain glint in the fading light.

Hours of wind, dusk in the hollows
where the deep roots crack in dryness like dead bones
in the sleep and shadow of the cold north light.

10TH AVENUE

1.

The sky descending red-streaked black and gray.
Faces blurred in windows, bus noise, bars, drunks in hallways.
A black woman, hair slicked back, whistling at the cold.

2.

Night shields him, a shadow beneath the streetlamp, bag in his hand.
It is possible to remain unnoticed, slowly limping forward,
walk the streets a solitary figure turning a corner.

3.

A city of accustomed dread, chain locks on the door.
The drunken Spanish nightshift stalking down blind alleys.
Old men, absence in the eyes, listing to a broken wall.

BLOCK ISLAND BLUES

Sunset: jaundiced, the sun
splashed into the sea
ebbing green and gray,
a tide of bilge and backwash
swelling tidal pools
with sewage, silt, and slush.

Dusk: adamant still, we kiss.
In this last night, sitting
on the mudflat beach,
we talk of love. Now night:
high above, circling seagulls
wail for water, for light.

CHRISTOPHER'S DREAM

In a midwinter night of air
muffled hard as wire
and shadows spined across
the bowed back of the moon,
he dreamed of a woman
rising from the dark water,
half-snake slither uncurling
below her delicate head,
mouth whispering his name,
open and feeding. He dreamed
of what she had become, daughter
and wife, in the green crest
of water as it looped around him
in coils like midwinter light
hunching chill over flesh
and bone, of skin and the dry
rubbing coddle of scales bristled
stiff in the wind, the face
nuzzling in darkness, the knowing
tongue and teeth at his throat.

Sleep together in a cleft of rock,
faces touching, hands wound
in darkness where the dream
unfolds its last uncertain hour
in vein, nerve and bone
and shadows surge deeper
into night, savoring the pale

spinning and slow shame
of light that sinks
into darkening water,
the hushed coiling
of bellies and mouths
into rings of cold stone.
Nothing else remains
to be carried away.
No rasp of skin or husk
of blood, no shaft of light
to crop the wind, no sound
or breath to scatter the silence
writhing by the sea.

The Shadow of Death on the Open Water

Rows of starfish stiffened
in the sun unfold
from ridge to ridge
with the slow pulsations
of silence and time.

Circles of wind
carry the cold weight
of clouds that thud
across the sky
like dark horses.

Black mouths locked open,
gaunt cormorants the color
of dust and burned weeds
dart through
the ocean's hollow eye.

The finned thing, hiding
its face in the sea's
scored rocks, casts
its silent and odorless
shadow on the open water.

Easter Morning

The boats rock clustered offshore,
cuffed by a cold spray of light
that begins nowhere and sluices
toward piers stiff as old veins
of grass in the hard chirr
of green water. The fishermen
have left on a rising wind,
from low tide and harbor flats
rankled by birds scything crabs
among the gray rocks, clearing
the tide line from the sand
as the sea retreats to Nantucket.

The wind is up and waves
flake the open tangle of kelp
and eelgrass beneath our feet.
We find our way across
the damp sags on this point of rock,
cutting low past the seawall
gaffed by winter on the edge
of this April morning, in silence
inexhaustible as water slipping
across the sand like shadows
of birds cast by a moon tacked
hard and white on the horizon.

The boats hover like gulls
half out to sea, tacking against

---

a sky shaken loose of clouds
and mottling with the wind
as it lifts to nets of light
that seine the water.
Under the surface, in the small
gray recesses of the birdless wall,
the dim grid of the season unlocks
in a voice that echoes like
a breaking wave swept to a sudden
formless blend of sky and sea.

Circles spread on the sand
as spring jabs the coast, foaming
with the tide through weeds
along the crest of the wall,
leaching salts that wrinkle
the damp places under the shoreline
stones and burrowing outward
in a familiar mix to tidal pools
hardening to sun. We huddle
in the wet sand below, traced
by a wicker of light and washed
by the cold absolution of water.

The boats fade with a shiver of wind
into the streaks of the eastern sky.
On shore this Easter morning,
above the line of thin-stemmed grasses
weaving slowly to the flicker of buds

on frail stalks, a knot of clawed tracks
of something born in the tidal marsh
leads to the darkened edge of the wall,
pausing here and there then spreading
unstoppable in all directions
like the hard snap of shadow
to sudden light that comes by water.

THE WHITE BEND OF THE RIVER

I.

Dead wood whitens
to connecting lines
that snap
with a brittle sting
as the season
dries to autumn.

Water the color
of charred sticks
stiff in the rain
beaks the clustered rocks,
thickening to knots of grass
that barb the horizon.

Drawn by the cradling wind
to the remains of summer,
you sleep in fitful starts,
weeping softly against me
long after the pain
has gone, dreaming

of a forgotten place
swept to silence by the river,
of children covered
in feathers
nuzzling the damp
smells of your body,

yourself, a whispered
shadow unspooling
in fields black
with birds, dragged
unraveling to the dull
white humming of water

where it flattens
to a thin cut around the bend,
its hoarse refrain
whiskering the sallow moon
as weeds spire and click
in the wind.

II.

Your hands are cold.
In this loose moment
of certainty between
dusk and the chill
anticipations of night
that rattle loose

like buried things
unearthed from the hollows
and old holes
lining the hard edges
of the river,
you tell me in whispers

about the thing
you are most afraid
to hear – the congested
flutter of birds
blinded by your
children struggling

in the shallows
among reeds and dredged
rocks, whipping murky
patches of water
to a swollen foam
of feathers and blood.

You are shadow
without light,
you say, the pale
deception of death
in this place
of resurrection,

a shred of darkness
that curls like
a shiver of fog above
the river whistling
anonymously into the gray
backwaters of night.

III.

Light appears suddenly
on the water,
brittle as glass
and the color
of dried feathers,
glances off old roots

straining against
the sear of wind
that jabs the grass
the way heat lightning
scuttles the stiff air
of late summer.

You finger sand
leeched to pallid streaks,
paring thin weeds
strung along the banks
like trapped birds
hobbled in effigy.

And I don't believe
you, even though
clouds wither
around us to
a residue that
stains the land

and the sky opens
in a penance of stars
spilling mutely
across the valley's
dim floor
and spinning outward

under the slow pulse
of your hand
as it trembles,
pure as a child's,
above the cold white
bend of the river.

IV.

It was the thing
you finally hoped for,
this congregation
of birds inching
through the grim
refractions of sky

on wings sharp
as the spines
of locust trees.
The air prickled
and shuddered
in their wake,

moving slowly at first,
then faster, lifting
branches of trees
bent with age
and chipped by
the scrape of winter.

You watched them
settle on the pulsing
surface of water,
clenched figures
floating into
changeable shapes, laced

to the river's twined
banks and dissolving
into radiant strands
of white feathers
that shimmer like silhouettes
on the blackening tide.

And you float gently
into the water, calling
out to the children,
bending your shadow
into the gathered corners
of this floundering night.

V.

The wind blows everywhere,
white and black, a hard
beaten wind that hisses
through the trees
along the river
in scorn and doubt.

The birds tumble
around you on wings
fragile as burned grass,
twisting above
the flat groan
and thud of water

toward some distant
invincible dead-center
without substance
or form, a whirlwind
of indifference
and desire

that whistles as it fills
the small cold darkness
where the ache
sets in and rattles
through the ruts and burrows
with the low sound

of your name in the vaulted
silence of this hour.
Time's blindness
broken by degree,
the marrow of light
spinning across the water

like things that do not move
then rise suddenly
in the endless symmetry
of birth and death giving
shape to the precipice
of river and air.

VI.

Time drifts past.
Only stones desire nothing.
The air is filled
with the sound of birds
murmuring of love
and despair.

The moon shines
on gray folds of mist
that thin and thicken
with a wind that blows
through the wallow
and ignorance

of the infinite stars,
through you, chilled
to the heart, through the endless
drift of transfigured shapes
that creak toward dawn
along the drab flats ahead.

The names of all we are,
all we have been
and known unravel
to simple bones
picked clean by birds
shaking with hope and pinned

among the flickers
of the day's last light.
The resolutions
of this shadowed hour.
The dry noise
of life to come.

The stars dissolve to dust
and the banks are awash
in a pale blue light
vacant as a sudden streak
of white against
the void of space.

VII.

the press and breath of silence
cool and dry as the dust
the flesh peels down to

the spindled slide of stillness into stillness
as midnight settles in against its hollow core
and the long night wanes to element and seed

salted in the natter and dream of birds
as the spirit comes to judgment turning
on itself at the iridescent edge of things

the field of being the white shore
where the end comes as a whisper on the wind
and light is transfigured to earth and air

the press and breath of silence
cool and dry as the dust
the flesh peels down to

the old confusion of water as the river skins
itself free of land where the moon
is hung and the wind whistles overhead

coalesced by sympathy and fire
to the ecstasy of hope in that deepest place
of undeciphered secret and stillborn sound

---

death and rising caged in the hull of time
of darkness gone and still to come
widening the chaos of the night sky

the press and breath of silence
cool and dry as the dust
the flesh peels down to

the shiver of wings stirring in message
or prayer untangled to writhing sinew
and luminous bone at the edge of the river

where the journey out of the self begins
with a distant chill and threads away
to echoes of wind and fluttering water

look   wings break with light
as birds stream out around you
in innocence in a cloud of white

CHIAROSCURO

A fine snow falls
across the harbor,
eats like white mold
into the darkness
that straddles the water
at Black Point.

Flaked with tiny pieces
of moon and knit
with dull mist,
the dark iced docks
wink in the distance
with the eyes of hooked gulls.

Wind churns the stiff reeds
and dry sea grasses
like a glistening
black hand laminated
with crusts
of chilled water.

Cold whittles
the raw wood of night,
huddles in the brittle
scraps of things
skinned black red
by the winter sea.

A sketch of white
curves past us back to shore
in predictable rhythms,
tilts to shade
across snow building
in the pale north.

And despite
this memory of loss,
your face is as hard
as rock chiseled
by the dim mottle of light
that pits the sea.

SIMPLE GESTURES

Tonight, as the air changes
and the light around
the dogwood fades
like the folding of old leaves,
I watch you press your face
against the window
and touch the cool glass
while evening bends
the deepening shadows
of the yard.

The years repeat themselves
in the perfect silence
of that simple gesture,
gentle as the soft scrape
of wild iris across the grass
in early summer,
and in the knowing lines
of your face, the clarity
of coming night
in a frame of pale hands.

A Point of Departure

The deep end of time
opens itself in the white ledge
and hush of branches
locked to the fragile
meditation of seeds.

This is the redemption
of hard weather
and reluctant light,
of hope discovered
in lengthening shadows,

in the pale bloom
of dust at dawn
that perfects
the landscape
as the journey begins,

in the music
of the spirit
returning in expectation
and wonder
on the determinate air.

Go now.
The sky
is washed in white
and night
yields the way.

Winter Geese

The changes of evening
come steadfast as birds
scraping the lake
in the darkness downwind.
A dim chill of light
tilts from the curve of water,
traces a black wave
of geese that lifts past
branches beyond our reach.
Winter comes this way
each year with the birds,
settling across the trees
and hard grass of the late
November hills as the season
turns toward the year's
darkness and softens
the sky to the colors
of weathered wood swollen
with the textures of wind.
Behind the dark windows
of this house,
tuned to the slide
of weather and not sure
of what it is we wait for
in all these long nights
of wind that whistles
through the cracks
of the chimney and repeats

the names of things
that we once were
softly, like some secret
hidden from itself,
I watched as night rippled
toward land in slow circles,
unraveling across the dark
fields to strings of cold rain,
and cried myself to sleep,
remembering in this music
of weather and wind
the empty places and
the dead silence of things
that pass like the circles
made by rain on still water
to the edges of shadows and dreams.
Now, as a thin layer
of frost coats rocks
stung with cold and stains
the roof and walls stitched
with the faint spume
of first light, I listen
in this ebb of time
between sleep and waking
to the whispers
of bitterness and sweet grief
in the folds of the wind,
shaking off again
the deep solitude of night
and the wearying press

of the painful emptiness
of this changing season
that even my remorse
at death could never fill.
Outside, incandescent as ice
in the first blue touch
of sunlight, the wild birds
trill the clear water
to a muffled, familiar sound.
One rises effortlessly
on white wings through
the misting lake grass
and hangs like slow smoke
on the horizon, circling home
to the white hills
in this half-light
like an unexpected sign
of hope plain against
the promised clearing
of this winter's dawn.

JONAS ZDANYS is a bilingual poet and the leading translator of modern Lithuanian literature into English. He has published thirty-seven other books, thirty-four of them collections of his own poetry, written in English and in Lithuanian, and of his translations of Lithuanian poetry and prose, for which he has received a number of prizes and book awards. He lives in North Haven, Connecticut.